Who Am I—
Knowing Your Identity in
CHRIST

Stephanie Gonzalez

ISBN 978-1-0980-8307-6 (paperback)
ISBN 978-1-0980-8308-3 (digital)

Christian Faith Publishing, Inc.
832 Park Avenue
Meadville, PA 16335
www.christianfaithpublishing.com

Printed in the United States of America

INTRODUCTION

Knowing who we truly are, our identity in Christ, will guide us to our purpose in life. Discovering the first part of the question answers the second. Finding our identity has been an age-old quest. As a child, I found my identity in who my parents said I was. As a teenager, I rejected that identity and tried to create my own identity. As a young adult, I began to return to who I was as a child, and as a new wife and young mother, I looked for my identity in my husband and children. Then as a young pastor, I threw my hands up, exasperated, and finally asked the One who created me. His answer was simple and liberating. His answer is the only one that matters in life because when I identify myself with who He says I am, all the other identities fall into place.

When God began speaking to me on the topic of my identity and revealing the importance of truly knowing and identifying myself as He does, I felt mandated to share with everyone I could this revelation. If anyone's opinion on who you are matters, it is Jesus's. And God's identity of you is most important. Want to know who you truly are? Let me answer that. When God sees you, He sees His child. It is as simple as that. When we understand this, truly making this our identity and who we see ourselves as, we will not fail in life. I pray that through this book, we will get a revelation like never before of who we are in Christ and understand what that means for us today.

CHAPTER 1

When a person incorrectly self identifies, it strips them of the authority God has given them. For example, if I hold a natural position as a company owner but I identify myself as an employee, then my behavior and my actions will always be of an employee. Look at Luke 15. Normally in this story, we focus on the prodigal son. We even call this parable the parable of the prodigal son. However, when it comes to the case of incorrect identity, let us look at his brother.

Luke 15:25 states, "Now, the older son was out working in the field when his brother returned…" Stop there. It points out that "the older son was out working in the field…" If we continue to verse 26, we will see that he calls over a servant to ask him a question, meaning this household had servants. It is easy to just read right through this, but if we stop and think about it from a business viewpoint, the question arises, Why was this son out in the field working? The household had servants or in modern language, the household had employees. We could speculate that perhaps the father (owner) made his son as a servant (employee) and that is why he was in the field working. But if we go back and read from verse 11, we will see that in verse 12, the father (owner) distributed his possessions to both brothers even though it was only the one who had asked for it. One brother asked for his inheritance, and the father divided it up and gave it to both, which would make the son who stayed behind and was working in the field the new owner. Look at verse 31 where the father (former owner) tells the older son, the one who was working in the field as an employee, that everything the dad has belongs to him. The owner was acting like an employee.

Why do I use this example? I believe one point Jesus was making in this story was that living with the wrong identity takes God-given authority away. The older son should have been in total authority over that household. Whatever crops that household produced should have been under this son's authority. Whatever income that household was making belonged to this older son, and he should have been using his authority to oversee and manage it. Instead, he was outside in the fields, acting like an employee. He was incorrectly self-identifying with a hired employee instead of the owner, and his actions, and quite frankly his attitude, followed.

If we incorrectly self-identify, it strips us of our God-given authority. When we should be acting like children of the Most High God, we have the attitude and actions of a sinner that is barely saved by grace. Where we should be stepping up and using our authority, we are taking a backseat and allowing things to happen in our lives that we should have authority over. Then when we do not like the outcome in our lives, we question God and His lack of intervention in this area. All along He is, like the dad in the story, saying, "Everything I have is yours." You use your authority to change the circumstance. Wow. God puts the ball in our court.

Just a few chapters earlier, in Luke 10:19, Jesus said:

> Now you understand that I have imparted to you all my authority to trample over his kingdom. You will trample upon every demon before you and overcome every power Satan possesses. Absolutely nothing will be able to harm you as you walk in this authority.

Psalm 24:1 says that God has claim over the earth and everything and everyone in it. When you accepted Jesus, you became an heir of God, joint heir with Christ (Romans 8:17). God has divided up His possessions (this earth) and given us authority in this world and over the circumstances within it.

When we do not live this life knowing our true identity, we live life lost and with no direction. Several years ago, I knew a person who was a very involved parent. When I say "very involved," I actually mean overly involved, as in everywhere her child was, she was there. Everything her child did, she did. As time passed, people around this mom noticed that her complete identity seemed to be in her role as a mom. Now for all of us moms, I believe we can identify with this mom and understand how she felt. As a mom of several kids, I know it can be easy to fall into the mom role.

Mom roles are kind of thrust upon you the moment that baby is conceived in your womb! Before baby is born, we are already doing things for him/her. When we run out for ice cream and pickles at midnight, we are already answering the beckoning call of that child! So I get it! Trust me, I have been there! But it is important that the mom identity does not replace who were truly are and who we were called to be. In this case, however, it was very obvious that this mom's identity was completely wrapped around her child. The problem started when that child became an adult, and the need for mom's daily input in life grew less and less. This left the mom searching for a new purpose, a new identity. Seemingly lost in this world, stripped of her day-to-day identity. It can be painful to watch a person who is lost and does not know where to place their identity. No one wants to come to a place in life where they no longer know who they are and feel lost in this world. Yet, so many in this life face this challenge, and the reason goes back to not correctly self-identifying.

Every role or part we play in this world is subject to change except the role as a child of God. When we identify ourselves with our role instead of who we are and that part changes, we become lost, and we lack direction. The children of Israel in the Bible are a good example of people whose roles changed, and in the change of identity, they lost their way. If we look at the book of Exodus, we see a people that were born into captivity, and their identity was that of a slave. They desired to leave their captivity and become a free people. However, as we read about their grand and eventful exit from Egypt, we begin to see how the further away they got from their captivity, the more lost they became. Their role in life changed from slaves

to free people, and they did not know how to function in this new identity.

Chapter 16:3 is just one example of the children of Israel's misplaced identity. At this point God, through Moses and Aaron, had brought them out of slavery, taken them from the identity of a slave, and they were now free people. However, their mentality, who they identified as, was still that of a slave. In verse 3, they complained to each other saying, "Oh, that we had died by the hand of the Lord in the land of Egypt, when we sat by the pots of meat and when we ate bread to the full! For you have brought us out into this wilderness to kill this whole assembly with hunger." In essence, they were complaining that they would have rather died in captivity where at least they had food than in freedom and hungry. That is the mentality of one who is comfortable in bondage.

Why would they have been more comfortable in slavery? Why would they have preferred to be fed slaves than hungry, free people? The answer is simple: all they had ever known was slavery. Their people had been in bondage for over four hundred years. It is what they knew; it is what they were comfortable with. It was their identity. Out in the wilderness, they had to use faith. They had to trust in their leader. In captivity, if they obeyed and did what they were told, then they survived. They did not have to trust the Egyptians, just obey them. These people faced an identity crisis the whole journey through the wilderness. They were lost, and it took them over forty years of wandering, lost, with no direction. What could have been basically a straight shot to their destination became a long, windy, difficult journey. I believe God knew these people needed some time to break free from the slavery identity they had adapted to. They were lost, not just physically in the wilderness but in their way of thinking and viewing themselves.

When talking about why knowing your true identity and who you are matters, we cannot overlook the area of salvation. We will only be absolutely confident in our salvation when we understand who salvation has made us. Let me explain. When we accept Jesus as our Lord and Savior, we automatically have an identity change. We are transformed from a slave to this earth to a free, blood-bought

child of God. However, just as the children of Israel, changing our image of ourselves to ourselves takes effort and in most cases, time. We must go from having the mentality of the world to having the mentality of a child of God.

As we develop the identity of a child of God, our assurance in our salvation becomes unshakable. Too many Christians still identify as a child of this world more than they do a child of God, and as history shows, behavior follows who we identify as. An all-A student is not okay with getting a C. It's almost painful for an all-A student to see a C on a test or report card. I have four daughters, and the first two are very self-motivated. They have been their whole lives. My oldest is especially driven to be the top of her class. She strives to get those A's at school. In the past, teachers have mentioned to me that maybe I shouldn't push too hard because they saw how hard she was on herself in class and assumed the pressure was coming from home. I had to assure them the pressure wasn't coming from us. I talked to my daughter and told her that if she got a B or C, as long as she did her best, it was fine.

The point was to do her best, not necessarily to get an A. It went in one ear and out the other because she saw herself as an A student. An all-A student identifies as an all-A student, and when that A is not there, they are not at peace. Likewise, a child of God who still identifies as "just a sinner saved by grace" will accept the behavior of a child of the world. They may not necessarily be pleased with sinful behavior, but they will be accepting of it because their identity is that of a sinner. However, when a child of God begins to identify as a child of God, then any behavior that does not exemplify the lifestyle of Jesus becomes unacceptable, almost painful.

As a child I grew up in a family of faith. My parents were pastors, and they didn't just "talk the talk" but they "walked the walk." We grew up living by faith, speaking by faith, and identifying as children of God. I am very blessed to have been raised in the family I was blessed with. The first lie I remember telling my dad was over a cassette tape! I had a cassette playing in my Walkman, and that tape was not a Christian artist. It was a tape full of love songs, one being too mature for a twelve-year-old girl to listen to, but I liked the music, bought the tape, and hid it from my parents! When my dad found it, which parents always will, and asked whose it was, I lied. I said it was my friend's tape and I had borrowed it. That lie was one of the most painful things I had ever done up to that point in my life! My stomach churned, and my head hurt! That lie was all I could think about the whole night!

My voice saying those words rang in my ears while I tried to forget about it and go to sleep! It was painful. Why did telling that lie hurt so much? It wasn't that big of a lie. One might call it a "white lie." Ah, but my identity was that of a child of God. Lying was not a part of my character because I was not brought up to identify with the world. Not that I was perfect or without sin, but it was not in my character because I was brought up to identify as a child of God, not a child of the world. A child of God is confident in their Father and that what He says is true. Therefore, a child of God is confident in their salvation. A person who truly identifies as a child of God will not go running to the altar a hundred times to renew their salvation. I'm not saying that's wrong. Do that if you need to be assured of your salvation, but at some point, we must stop identifying as a child of the world, full of sin, and unworthy of His love, and start identifying as a child of God, redeemed because of His love, and worthy of His love because of what He did for us! Jesus bought and paid for our salvation, and until we identify as God's own, we will always feel unworthy when He has made us worthy!

When we do not identify ourselves correctly—a child of God— then we will not expect as much for ourselves as we should. When life blows us a bad deal, we will be more accepting of it if we identify with being children of the world rather than children of God. Tough times hit or we are faced with tragedy, and our response is, "That's life." We settle for far too much junk that life throws at us when we should stand in our position as children of God and just as Jesus did the natural storm in life (Matthew 8:26), speak to the bad situation, and make it stop. As mentioned earlier in the chapter, we will not recognize our authority if we do not know who we are. We will accept a lower standard in life for ourselves and from ourselves.

Children of the world take what the world gives them. Children of God take what God gives them. We must know who we are in Christ.

I believe Jesus is our perfect example of one who strived at knowing who He was. When we read His story, we see times when Jesus emphasized the need in His life to learn who He was, and I believe there are many more times that are not recorded. I believe Jesus's main goal up until the time of His ministry was discovering who He was as the Son of God. Imagine the thoughts that ran through His head as His mother, Mary, told Him of the angel visiting her to announce His soon arrival and of His family's journey to escape King Herod when He was just a toddler. Imagine the excitement He felt hearing the prophecies of Isaiah and relating Himself as the one to fulfill them.

He had to learn His position on earth as the Son of God. I am sure He had this inner longing to know more of God and find out what authority He was given. At the age of twelve, He sat in the temple with scholars and doctors and men who had devoted their lives to studying God while His parents journeyed home. He was separated from His parents, but His hunger to know more of God and really, more of Himself and His purpose caused Him to sit for at least two days in that temple, talking and listening to the teachings of the prophets and of His Father.

Several times throughout Jesus's ministry, we see Him separate Himself to get alone with God, I believe, consulting with God, seeking God's will, and discovering more and more of His purpose on earth. Jesus could not face death, the grave, and hell if he did not know who He was. Only someone confident in His position in the kingdom and with His Father could endure such torture and pain, someone convinced of His role to play in the kingdom of God. Resurrection could not take place unless He was confident in His authority as the Son of God and in God's love for Him. I believe in the pits of hell He cried out Psalm 16:10, "For You will not leave my soul in Sheol, nor will You allow Your Holy One to see corruption."

As children of God, our desire should be to seek out what our purpose in the kingdom of God is. Like Jesus, we should be spending time learning more about God, our authority as children of God, and our purpose in His kingdom! We must know who we are in Christ, what authority has been given to us, and what our purpose is. Like Jesus, we should have the confidence in the midst of a life storm, in the midst of all hell breaking loose, we can stand up and boldly say, "You will not leave my soul in hell!" and "Peace be still."

Knowing who we are is not automatic once we get saved. Everything God says we are, everything He says we have is available to us the moment we receive salvation, but it is not activated in our lives until we activate it. And we cannot activate something we do not know about. It is similar to a relative leaving us a million dollars in a bank account with our name on it. If we do not know about that million dollars, it does us no good. If we do not understand that we are the beneficiary of that million dollars, that it is our name on the bank account, and only by our authority can it be accessed, then that million dollars will sit in that account and do no good for us. It is unused power, an unused tool to better people in this life. How many of us have unused, God-given power and tools to make life better for ourselves and more importantly, for others because we didn't take the time as Jesus did to study the Word of God and discover ourselves, our roles, our purpose in this life?

We must know who we are in Christ. We must seek our purpose as Jesus did and desire to fulfill it each and every day. We must not just read about our authority and positioning in the kingdom of God but identify with it as it becomes our very own nature and character as children of God. When we establish our identity and see ourselves the way God sees us—as His children—we will become so much more effective in the kingdom of God. We will love the way Jesus loved, serve the way He served. We will sacrifice the way He sacrificed, and be fulfilled the way He was fulfilled. Let our goal in life be to discover His plan and His purpose for our lives and raise our standard of living for ourselves and from ourselves, having direction and goals, and walking in our full authority.

CHAPTER 2

This world will automatically label us and try to put identities on us—where we have come from, who we associate with, our roles in life, and what we can do for them. It is natural for others to try to pinpoint our identity. It is how we learn to view others. Unfortunately, if we are not confident in who we are, we will take the labels and identities that other give us and adapt our lives to those identities. Everyone born in this world will be given multiple identities, but if we are aware of this, then we will choose to self-identify with the identity that God gives us.

Jesus wasn't exempt from being labeled with false identities either. While in this world, the world tried to identify Him or place its own identity on Him. I love this short scripture that mainly goes unnoticed in the book of John. In John 1:43–45, we find Jesus in Galilee meeting Philip and calling him out as a disciple. Galilee was not considered the place where the most holy came from. In fact, Isaiah referred to it as "the land of gentiles" (Isaiah 9:1–2). Galileans were not considered the most educated and polished of the Jews. In fact, in Acts 2:7, we see where people from all over the Middle East were gathered and heard the disciples speaking in their native tongues, and their response was, "Aren't these all Galileans?" (verse 7), as if to imply that they should not be educated enough to speak these foreign languages. In fact, according to The Passion Translation footnote for John 1:46, Galileans were considered "backward people."

Perhaps Nazareth, a city in Galilee, was considered even more as a backward, country-bumpkin place. We can assume this because of a man named Nathaniel's response in verse 46 of John 1. Philip runs to get Nathaniel, who seems to be a man seeking God, and tells him that they have found the Messiah, the one they have been waiting for: a man named "Jesus, son of Joseph of Nazareth!" (Verse 45). Nathaniel's response gets me every time. Verse 46 says, "Nathanael sneered, 'Nazareth! What good thing could ever come from Nazareth?' Philip answered, 'Come and let's find out!'" Here is Jesus minding His own business, calling out disciples, and Nathaniel immediately identifies Him with where He came from, His childhood roots.

Imagine if Jesus would have identified Himself with where He came from—an unsophisticated country boy from Nazareth. What if when Mary told Him of His miraculous birth and the prophecy of the angel, He had responded with, "Not me, Mom. I'm just a kid from Nazareth. Why would God use me?!" Jesus had to identify with who God said He was! He had to know who He was and everything that entailed! How many times have we been labeled because of where our roots are? How many times have we limited ourselves because we know where we came from? "I'm just a kid from South Texas. Why would God use me?" When we identify ourselves from God's viewpoint, as His children, those labels, those sub standards are lifted!

Jesus was also identified and labeled by His association. In the latter part of Matthew 13, we see where the "church folk" or people in the temple were baffled at His wisdom and knowledge. They asked in verses 55 to 56, "Isn't He just the wood-worker's son? Isn't his mother named Mary, and his four brothers Jacob, Joseph, Simon, and Judah? And don't his sisters all live here in Nazareth? How did he get all this revelation and power?" People did not understand Jesus's authority because they were identifying Him with his earthly family instead of His heavenly Father. We see the results of this incorrect identification in verse 57 when they became offended at Him because He was speaking above His natural position in life. In their mind He was the carpenter's boy speaking as a temple scholar, and that offended them. Have we ever found ourselves in this position? We share the Word as we have studied it, but it was received in offense because the revelation we have is above our "family status!"

The life-changing Rev. Billy Graham grew up on a dairy farm in Charlotte, North Carolina. Imagine if when he felt the call to preach, he had thrown out the excuse to God, "But I'm just a boy from a dairy-farming family." Imagine if his identity was wrapped up in his family roots and not in his heavenly Father! Would he have fulfilled his purpose? How many thousands of people would not be in heaven or heading that way because he felt too unqualified to carry out God's calling on his life? I believe many people have missed out on fulfilling their purpose because they identified themselves with who they came from instead of WHO they belong to.

Many times we identify ourselves with our career or position, the roles we play in life. My husband and I help oversee a Christian school out of our church, and for the past ten years, we have held the position as principals. Once, several years ago, one of our kindergarten students saw us in the evening at Chick-fil-A and shouted out, "Hey, Principal, why did you leave the school?" In her mind, we lived at the school 24-7. To her, that was our identity, that is who we were and nothing else. She seemed almost upset at the fact that we were not at the school! Sometimes we get caught up in our careers or our positions in life, and that becomes our identity. Granted people will identify us with what we do, I'm not denying that. But the trouble begins when we begin identifying ourselves as our careers or positions in life.

We can see this effect in seniors who retire early. According to a study done on former Shell Oil employees, those who retired at fifty-five and lived to sixty-five died younger than those who continued working and retired at sixty-five. Why would we see this happen? In my opinion, it is due to the loss of identity, loss of purpose. When someone identifies themselves with what they do or what position they hold and that job or position is gone, they no longer have their identity and become lost, as chapter one covered, in this world.

Our calling in the ministry is not any different. Many times we try to justify our identity in our calling. A person who is called as a missionary and finds themselves wrapped up in the identity of a missionary may not be able to find their way once they are no longer capable of being out in the missions field. In my lifetime, I have seen many people called to ministry as pastors, missionaries, and evangelists who have allowed their identity to became wrapped up in their calling. And when the position is no longer available or God sends them into a new chapter in life, they become lost and are left with a feeling of hopelessness.

Our identity should not be our calling or our career. That may be one aspect of our identity, but once again, we must choose to identify ourselves with our true identity and that is a child of God. Being a child of God is the one identity that is not subject to change in this life. Every other identity may come and go, but being a child of God is steady and unchangeable. It does not depend on any outer source, and it does not depend on anything we do or do not do. Identifying as a child of God grounds us and gives us roots that will not be taken away. If we lost everything in life, like Job in the Bible, we will still have our foundation, our true identity of being a child of God.

In this chapter, we are covering who the world says we are and how they identify us. One of the ways that the world identifies us is by what we can do for them. We see this too often in intimate relationships that end up going bad because identity is placed in what one can do for the other. As a pastor, I have heard my share of "I just don't love him/her anymore," when justifying divorce. While we could get into the nitty gritty of just how false this "feeling" is, the truth is if we see each other the way God sees as—as children of God—then there is no "falling out" of love.

The problem is we identify one another on what they can do for us or how they make us feel. Instead, we should be seeing one another as children of God and part of the family of Jesus. Identities that are based on actions or behaviors are misplaced and very unsteady, and we view who we are based on what we can bring to the table, and we will fall short. If I base my identity as a pastor and my ability to preach, then every time I feel like I did not deliver a sermon the way I thought I should, I will feel inadequate and disappointed. However, if my identity is placed as a child of God, even if I fail at what I do, I will still have my confidence. A person whose identity is in Christ may fail at what they do, but that does not change who they are.

Once I told my husband I thought I should preach the Christmas service message. Now Christmas service is considered one of the most important services, largest in attendance, and most anticipated church services in the year. For some, this and Easter are the only two services they'll attend, so pastors around the world want to be sure they get in a good God-given message for their Christmas service. So taking on this responsibility was not an easy task. I studied. I sought God. I prayed. I fasted! And I believed I had the Word of the Lord for that day! I was excited! I was ready to share God's love through the Word on that Christmas service day!

Service began, and just as expected, it was a packed house. The children sang their beautiful Christmas songs. The Praise Team added a few carols to their list of worship songs. Everything was beautiful, and I was ready! As I stood at the front and thanked everyone for joining us, my mind went blank. I looked at my notes, and they all seemed to blur together! What should have been a forty-five-minute message ended in twenty-five! I missed my main points. My "amen" moments fell on a silent crowd. When I wrapped it up (early), I walked to my seat and held in my tears. What had happened? What did I do wrong? My nerves got the best of me. Maybe I didn't prepare enough. Maybe I should have gone over my notes two hundred times instead of just one hundred. My thoughts raced. I went home, got alone with God, and repented. *I messed it all up*, I told him. *My message today was a flop, and I feel like I dishonored you on the most important service of the year.*

I felt like a failure as a minister, a wash-up as a pastor. In the silence, in my room, I heard the Lord speak to me and say, *Who are you?*

I answered, *I'm Stephanie.*

He asked again, *No, who ARE you?*

Again, I answered, *I'm Stephanie. Jaime's wife, pastor, mom, principal——*

He stopped me there and said as gentle as could be, *No. Those are hats you wear, but they are not who you are. You are MY CHILD, my daughter. You may fail at times wearing those other hats, but you will NEVER fail as my child.*

Wow, what a rush of relief filled my heart and mind at that moment. Knowing that my true identity was fail-proof. I couldn't mess it up. I would always be a child of the King, and nothing and no one could change that! Peace filled my thoughts, and I was able to smile at my imperfect message delivery that day, and instead of moping around about it, decided to figure out what went wrong and fix it for the next time. God's love and acceptance as His child are so amazing, and that is why this message of knowing who we are is so important. It will take us from being failures in life to being a success. Knowing who we are, our true identity in life, will help us in every area of our lives. Instead of wallowing in our failures, we will take mishaps and turn them into learning experiences. We won't be hopeless or lost, but we will confidently know that no matter what areas we may fail in, there is one that we cannot mess up and that is being children of God. He accepts and loves us just the way we are!

CHAPTER 3

W̲e have discussed who the world says we are and how the world identifies us. In this chapter, we will cover who God says we are and how He identifies us. In 1 Peter 2:9 NKJV, the author states, "But you are a chosen generation, a royal priesthood, a holy nation, His own special people…" I want to focus on the "chosen generation" part of this scripture.

As children of God, we are chosen. One of the definitions of the word "chosen" by Webster's 1828 dictionary, is "distinguished by preference." When we put this into perspective of God choosing us, this is powerful! God distinguished us by His preference! That means He picked us out because He preferred us, He loved us. He looked at everyone and pointed at me and said, "I pick this one. She is my favorite," and He did that to each of us individually. Each one of us is His preferred one, His favorite, His chosen! He loves every single one of us and has called us, "Chosen."

Jesus said in John 15:16, "You didn't choose me, but I've chosen and commissioned you to go into the world to bear fruit." Read that again, "You didn't choose me, but I've chosen…you." We are chosen of God, hand-picked and called His own! That alone gives us a reason to live. When we fully understand the fact that God has chosen us and our identity is in Him and not in ourselves, we should be unbreakable, unshakable, and ready to take on this world! What else could we possibly need other than being chosen by God? What else can compare to being His child, His chosen one? This isn't something that is just given to ministers or those who dedicate their lives to preaching His Word. This is something that we all are partakers of! He picked me; He picked you; we are CHOSEN!

In addition to being chosen by God, we are anointed! Many people see the word "anointed" and automatically think that this is a reference to ministers of the Gospel. While ministers do fall under this category as well, we might be surprised to find that each one of God's children are anointed. There are different anointing, and with the giftings God has placed in our lives, the anointing will follow. As pastors, my husband and I often look to find the giftings placed in people's lives. We have seen that when you find a person's giftings, you will see the anointing follow in that area. For example, we have seen people who are amazing at caring for children. They literally love being around children, and children flock to them like they were the Pied Piper! Children of all ages love them, from infants to teen-agers! It is amazing! They have a gift for working with children, and with that gift comes the anointing to work with children.

We have seen the gift of cooking. Yes, cooking! One member in our church is flat-out gifted to cook. We could literally call her at midnight and ask her to cook a meal for three hundred people by lunch tomorrow, and it would be done. And it would be done well! The food would be on time, and it would taste great, and she would have fun the whole time she was preparing the food. She has a gift to cook with that, she has an anointing to cook.

God has anointed each of us in some area in life. 2 Corinthians 1:21a says, "Now, it is God himself who has anointed us..." Until we find that area that God has anointed us in, we will feel unfulfilled and unsatisfied in life. Now I must go back to chapter 2 and reiterate that this anointing is a complement to our calling. But this calling is not our identity! It may be how many identify us, but it is not the way we should identify ourselves. Our calling is a complement to who we are, which, once again, is a child of God! We must not con-fuse our calling and what we are anointed to do as our identity! We are chosen because God loves us, plain and simple.

As children of God, we have been made righteous. We will go more in depth on this topic in Chapter 5, but I cannot cover who

God says we are without covering righteousness. 2 Corinthians 5:21 says:

> For He [God] made the only One [Jesus] who did not know sin to become sin for us, so that we who did not know righteousness might become the righteousness of God through our union with Him.

Jesus became sin so we could become righteous, both of which neither of us had been! This is one of those scriptures that is hard to grasp when we don't self-identify as children of God. We know our imperfections, our thoughts, and our behavior. We have dealt with our attitudes, our cynicism, and our failures. So to identify as being righteous is a bit of a stretch for most of us. But this scripture says that because of our union with Christ, we are made righteous just as truly as Jesus was made sin on that cross.

This scripture doesn't say if we feel righteous, then we are righteous or if we are good enough, then we are made righteous. Jesus did not have to do anything to become sin. In fact, He didn't do anything to become sin. He did not sin; He did no wrong whatsoever. What He did do was the opposite of sin! He gave His own life to become sin. And this scripture likens our becoming righteous to that of Jesus becoming sin. Still, we inertly feel like we must do something to become righteous. We must do better, we must stop a bad habit, we must go to church more often, and other stipulations mankind has put on being righteous. We try to earn righteousness, and righteousness is not something that can be earned—it is something given. "Because of our union with Him," we are made righteous. The more we identify with who God says we are, the more we will understand righteousness and realize that what we believed to be mandatory actions or behaviors to become righteous were actually products of righteousness and knowing who we are in Christ Jesus.

God says we are His. Isaiah 43:1 New King James Version says, speaking to Israel, "Fear not, for I have redeemed you; I have called you by your name; You are Mine." Because of redemption on the cross, we are included in this scripture! *When we gave our life to Christ and became born-again, we entered into the household of faith!* Therefore, we have been called by name. We are His! God calls us His! What does this mean? It means we have direct communion with God the Father, the Creator of heaven and earth. We have direct access to His throne room, and we have communion with Him. Communion means "fellowship." So, we have fellowship with Him! Because He has called us by name and we are His, then we have fellowship with the Father! This means that we can talk directly to the God of the Universe, the Creator of all things! But if we are not identifying as a child of God, if our identity is in what we do or who others say we are or whatever hat we are wearing for the day, then we will not realize the right and privilege we have as His children.

To be able to talk to and commune with God is such a vital part of our lives and the life that the Father wants us to live. He desires communion with us. He wants to hear our thoughts, our prayer or just how our day went! That is what relationship is about and that is what communion entails! But again, if we are not identifying ourselves correctly and seeing who He says we are, then we will not have the boldness to talk with God the way He desires. God loves us so much that He gave everything so that we could have fellowship or communion with Him. If we are still living and acting as though we are unworthy of this relationship with Him, then we are counting the cross as not enough, and let me just say, the cross was more than enough!

CHAPTER 4

———— ⌒⌒ ————

Redemption—so much wrapped up in one word! Webster defines redemption as "deliverance from bondage." Redemption is also forgiveness, but in addition to forgiveness, it is the "wiping away from the consequence of the wrong done." Redemption took place on the cross! By becoming sin for us, Jesus not only made a way for our sin to be forgiven but for the penalty of sin to be removed from us. He took on not only the sin but the price or wage of sin.

The wage of sin is death (Romans 6:32), but Christ Jesus paid that price for our sin, which was His death. But not only did He pay the price, He also bought redemption for us all! Now because of Jesus, we are free from the law of both sin and death (Romans 8:2). We are free from the bondage of sin and death! We have been given the promise of eternal life, meaning after physical death. We enter into a marvelous life that cannot even be imagined!

I love the sonnet-like scripture in 1 Corinthians 15:55–56, "So death, tell me, where is your victory? Tell me death, where is your sting?" We can boldly say this because verse 56 tells us, "It is sin that gives death its sting and the law that gives sin its power." Sin no longer has power over us because Jesus became sin and redeemed us from its consequence.

But pastor I still sin, we may say. Yes, but Jesus took care of sin on the cross, and the more we identify as His redeemed children, the less pull sin has in our lives! If, however, we still identify with being "just human," the more pull sin will have on our lives. Remember in Chapter 1 the example of the all-A student? A student who sees themselves as an all-A student will never be satisfied with getting B's and C's. Children of God who identify as children of God will never be satisfied with sin in their lives. Their standard for living will be higher than that of a sinner saved by grace. This is why it is so important that we view ourselves the way God sees us—as His children!

Redemption also frees us from fear! If we look once again at the New King James Version of Isaiah 43:1, it declares, "Fear not, for I have redeemed you..." We have been redeemed from fear! As children of God, we have a right not to fear! This isn't something common to mankind. *Fear comes naturally, but freedom from fear comes supernaturally!*

As we identify more with the supernatural us, as children of God, and less of just mankind, then we will begin to realize we have power over fear and power over the evil and danger in this world. Jesus, who knew in His heart that He was the Son of God, despite what the world said, was able to face the deadliest of situations and not fear.

In Matthew 8, Jesus and His disciples got into a fishing boat to cross a lake. Jesus, being tired, fell asleep. Verse 24 says, "Suddenly a violent storm developed, with waves so high the boat was about to be swamped." I'll stop right there to say I think this is a time when no one would have judged Jesus for feeling a little scared! But the verse goes on to say, "Yet Jesus continued to sleep soundly." What? Here is a moment when any natural person would be afraid! This is essentially a life-or-death situation! Yet Jesus slept on! I am sure the disciples looked at Jesus, thinking, "Why aren't you scared?" and Jesus looked at them and replied, "Why are you?" I love that response!

In a time when any natural person would be afraid, He continued to stay in rest, and His response was "Why are you afraid?" This is Jesus who had learned and was still learning who He was. He was confident in His identity as The Son of God. This is what our Father desires of us—that we become confident in who we are in Him! Then when situations arise that would normally throw us into a panic, we can remain calm and continue to rest through the storm!

In 2019, when my mom was diagnosed with cancer in her reproductive system, instantly, fear tried to take over my mind. Thoughts from all over the place began bombarding my thinking, and being a Word pastor and being raised in a Word pastor's home, I immediately fought these thoughts. I knew better than to allow them to become by meditation. When I spoke to my mom, she very calmly told me, "I'm not afraid." She knew and knows what the Word says, and she knows who she is in Christ and that what the Word says belongs to us, we truly can have.

The Bible says in Isaiah 53:5b that "in His wounding, we found out healing." New King James says, "by His stripes, we are healed." When we know who we are in Christ Jesus, as children of God, then we will be confident that what the Word says we have access to, we can have in our lives! Then scriptures like Isaiah 53:5 rings true in our hearts that we are healed! Redemption brings freedom from sickness because it brings revelation of healing! Our confidence in His Word gets stronger in our hearts and minds. Healing belongs to the children of God. The problem occurs when we do not identify ourselves as the children of God but instead we find our identity in the world or in natural humanity. It is then that we do not feel worthy of supernatural healing. Our natural health depends on our confidence in our supernatural right to healing!

As children of God, we are redeemed from our past. That is one very powerful statement for all of us! In my opinion, everyone has something in their past that they are not proud of! One of the devil's tools that he uses against us is identifying us with our past. His goal is to keep us chained to our past identity and the darkness it holds! But Jesus has redeemed us from our past!

Second Corinthians 5:17 declares, "Now, if anyone is enfolded into Christ, he has become an entirely new creation. All that is related to the old order has vanished. Behold, everything is fresh and new." I love The Passion Translation's footnote on this scripture. It states, "This would include our old identity, our life of sin, the power of Satan, the religious works of trying to please God, our old relationships with the world, and our old mind-sets. We are not reformed or simply refurbished, we are made completely new by our union with

Christ and the indwelling Holy Spirit." Wow! What a description of what being a new creation means!

In other words, we are made completely new! Our former identity is gone. We have a new identity, which brings a new standard for living and a new scale to judge ourselves on! We are made new. Thank you, Jesus! Anyone with anything in their past that they are not proud of can shout, "Hallelujah!" We are not held accountable anymore for that old identity! Our slate has been thrown out, burned up, and we have been given a new slate! If only people living for the world truly understood this concept. If only believers dealing with guilt and shame of their past fully understood this scripture!

Redemption brings freedom from our past and gives us our new identity in Him! We are no longer connected to our former identity! We are free. A scripture to meditate on is Ephesians 1:7: "Since we are now joined to Christ, we have been given the treasures of redemption by his blood—the total cancellation of our sins—all because of the cascading riches of his grace." Redemption is "the total cancellation of our sins!"

CHAPTER 5

———— ✑ ————

Grace is one of those powerful multifaceted words like redemption! We cannot talk about self-identifying correctly without talking about grace! One of the definitions given by Webster's 1928 Dictionary is "the application of Christ's righteousness to the sinner." Really think about what that description is saying. It is Christ's righteousness applied to the sinner! The righteousness of Jesus applied or poured onto the sinner! It gets more powerful each time we rephrase that!

When I read that definition, I picture a large jar of oil representing the righteousness of Christ being poured onto the head of a sinner, covering every square inch of that person until you cannot see the flesh as it is drenched in the oil of grace! This is what God sees when He looks at me and you! He sees us, and He sees the righteousness of Christ!

Second Corinthians 5:21 says, "For God made the only one who did not know sin to become sin for us, so that we who did not know righteousness might become the righteousness of God through our union with him." Jesus became sin so we could become His righteousness! So when the Father sees us, He sees Jesus! He sees us through the eyes of grace! *If God who created the universe sees us as righteous, what a false identity we have seeing ourselves as helpless sinners!* When we do not see ourselves as children of God, then we are not identifying with the cross and all that Jesus endured on that cross to make us righteous! We are discrediting Jesus's sacrifice! Let that sink in! We think we are being humble in viewing ourselves as less than righteous when, in fact, we are discounting the greatest sacrifice ever made.

Grace has given us a new identity, the identity of Jesus. Grace liberates us from the bondage of sin! It says, "No matter what you have done, my grace covers it!" The Lord says through Paul in 2 Corinthians 12:9, "My grace is always more than enough for you…" Grace is more than enough for our downfalls! Instead of hiding in our sin, as Adam and Eve did in the Garden of Eden, we can come boldly to the throne of God and His forgiveness and grace! But of course, if we do not see ourselves through the eyes of grace of our Father sees us, then we will not have the confidence to enter into forgiveness.

When we identify with grace, as a child of God, then we have the assurance of acceptance. Our confidence in God's love grows the more we find who we are in Him. We will have an assurance of being His when we know who we are in Him. With this assurance, our confidence in ourselves increases, and our confidence to share Him with others expands. We find the explanation of our acceptance in Ephesians 1:5–6:

> For it was always in His perfect plan to adopt us as His delightful children, through our union with Jesus, the Anointed One, so that His tremendous love that cascades over us would glorify His grace—for the same love He has for His Beloved One, Jesus, He has for us. And this unfolding plan brings Him great pleasure!

The New King James Version ends that scripture with "He made us accepted in the Beloved." When we received Jesus, we were adopted as God's children, and this scripture says, "the same love He has for Jesus, He has for us." Revelation of that scripture is enough to free us from the enslavement of sin! God loves us like He loves Jesus! That sounds like acceptance to me! We are "accepted in the Beloved!" But a free person is only free if they know and identify with being free.

When we truly understand that God's love for us is uncondi-
tional and without limits, it liberates us from always seeking to please
God with our vain works and religious attitudes. His love is pure and
simple. It is a gift. We did not earn it, and we cannot be good enough
for it or bad enough to lose it. Nothing we can do will make Him
love us less or more. Nothing we can do will make Him reject us.
Only we can reject God by doubt and unbelief. Trusting in this love
will ignite in us a love for Him that gets stronger as relationship with
Him gets stronger and confidence in Him gets stronger. The more
we know Him, the more we love Him, and the more we love Him,
the more we desire to please Him. Sin loses its hold on us when we
bask in His love. Frustration and depression cannot reside in a person who understands God's love and acceptance for them. When we
know we are accepted, we will know who we are in Him.

Having a revelation of God's love and acceptance for us assures
within us our forgiveness of sin. The second part of Romans 3:24
declares, "His gift of love and favor now cascades over us, all because
Jesus, the Anointed One, has liberated us from the guilt, punishment, and power of sin!" We are "liberated" from sin! And not just
from sin but from the guilt of sin, the punishment of sin, and the
power of sin! We are no longer guilty of sin because of Jesus!

Sin's grip has no power over us unless we allow it to. The way
we allow sin to still have power over us it when we do not know who
we are in Him, when we do not know our identity in Christ, when
we self-identify incorrectly. Then the condemnation of sin has rule in
our lives. And when we mess up, we allow guilt and shame to cause
us as it did to Adam in the garden of Eden, to want to hide from
God and run from Him rather than to Him. What Christ did on
that cross enables us to run straight to Him when we mess up, but if
we do not have this understanding, then our human nature will be
to run away and hide.

Further in this passage, verse 27 explains that it is not our works
that bring God's acceptance, but it is our faith. Many believers strive
to do good in order to bring God's love and acceptance when all
along we should be building our faith in Him and strengthening
our understanding of our identity in Him! Only then we will have

assurance of our forgiveness based on Jesus's sacrifice and not based on anything we can do to earn it.

Dependency on Christ comes with knowing our identity. God desires our full reliance on Him because He is the ultimate caretaker! He has taken care of all our needs and desires! Whatever we have need of, Jesus already bought and paid for it on the cross! Second Peter 1:3 says that "everything we could ever need for life and complete devotion to God has already been deposited in us by His divine power."

In my life, I have never lacked anything. Sure, there are times I have wanted something and didn't have the means to get it, but I have a revelation that within me is the power and ability to have everything I need! If I truly want or need something and I put my faith out to get it, I will have it. My confidence is in a caretaking God, and He cares about the little and big things we want because He cares for us.

Recently, while quarantined through the Covid-19 pandemic, I sat on my porch feeling very emotional and lonely. I had my family with me, but I missed our church family and felt I could not be there for them in a time of crisis and need! I had a hopeless feeling, a feeling that I was not and could not do enough to help. I felt frustrated at being unable to go wherever I wanted to go and do whatever I wanted to do. God's gentle voice spoke to me during that time and He asked me, *Who is your support?* Immediately, I thought of everyone who would normally be there to help me with whatever task I was working on—my co-laborers at church, my "village" that helps me with my kids, my extended family that is there when I am in need—and then I quieted my thoughts and remembered that He is my ultimate support. He is the one that will never leave me (Hebrews 13:5)! He is my ultimate caretaker and honestly, the only One I need.

A person who does not know who they are in Christ will not understand this concept. They will seek the support of those around them, and their dependency on God will fall short. But for the one who knows who they are in Christ Jesus, they will always depend on Him as their ultimate support! Second Corinthians 12:9 states, "My grace is always more than enough for you, and my power finds its full expression through your weakness." The end of verse 10 is so powerful, "For my weakness becomes a portal to God's power." It is when we realize that our total dependency should be on God because we are not enough, but His grace is that He is able to manifest His power through us!

CHAPTER 6

In Chapter 5, we read a little bit about righteousness. Before talking about being a child of God and what all that entails, we must be convinced of our righteousness in Him. I love Romans 3:24. It says:

> Yet through his powerful declaration of acquittal, God freely gives away his righteousness. His gift of love and favor now cascades over us, all because Jesus, the Anointed One, has liberated us from the guilt, punishment, and power of sin!

The word *acquittal* means being declared not guilty, or as defined by *Webster's Dictionary*, "a deliverance from the charge of an offense." This scripture then starts off by letting us know that by declaration of the Ultimate Judge, we have been declared not guilty and delivered from even the charge of an offense! In other words, God has already judged us and called us innocent. Because of the cross, He is no longer judging us! The final judgement was on Jesus when He became sin for us. His price freed us from the bondage and consequence of sin.

The scripture goes on to say that "God freely gives away his righteousness." He has given us His righteousness. As mentioned before, there is nothing we have done to earn it, and there is nothing we ever could do to earn it. We cannot be good enough, smart enough, or giving enough to earn His righteousness. The only way we could have received His righteousness is if God gave it. There was no other way that we can become righteous. We were given the gift of God's righteousness, and we were given the gift of love and favor! The scripture says it "cascades over us."

When I read this, I picture myself standing under a waterfall in one of the beautiful islands of Hawaii! Water pouring over me to the extent that I am covered with a curtain of water! I am being drenched by the cool fresh flowing water! That is the picture I see when I think of God's love and favor cascading over me! His love covers us, washes us, renews us, and refreshes us!

The scripture finishes by declaring that "Jesus, the Anointed One, has liberated us from guilt, punishment, and power of sin!" If we were not convinced of being free from sin before, this scripture's ending states it very boldly. In the first part of the scripture, we were declared innocent of sin. And in the ending, we have been freed from the "guilt, punishment, and power of sin," not only free from sin itself but from the effects of sin in our life: the guilt and shame it brings, the punishment that comes with it, and the stronghold or power of sin! Once again, we are free from sin and the effects of it in our lives! Thank you, Jesus!

As we study and meditate on this scripture, that reality becomes truer in our hearts and minds, and we become liberated from condemnation of sin. When we are convinced of this scripture in our lives, then we will identify more as His children and not children of the world always striving to do good to gain His acceptance.

As we view ourselves as His children, our character and behavior will follow. We allow ourselves to act as His children, walking in full authority of a believer. When we walk in confidence of His love and acceptance, then we will not have to "try" not to sin. Sin will become detestable to us. It won't sit well within us because we know who we are, and we know whose we are. We will "make God our utmost pleasure and delight" and in return He will "provide" what we "desire most" (Psalm 37:4).

As children of God, all our needs are provided for. Philippians 4:19 states that "God will fully satisfy every need." When we do not identify as a child of God, this is a hard scripture to receive. However, when we know who we are, then we will fully believe and trust in this scripture. We will understand that there is no need too great for our loving Father!

Identifying as children of God also causes us to identify as heirs of God! Heirship is very important when knowing your identity. Christ died for us and in that death gave us the legal right to heirship. When one is an heir, that means they inherit everything that belonged to their predecessor. Jesus was the ultimate owner, and in His death, we became heirs to all He has and is. One of the definitions of an heir is "one who is entitled to possess." Romans 8:17 says:

> And since we are his true children, we qualify to share all his treasures, for indeed, we are heirs of God himself. And since we are joined to Christ, we also inherit all that he is and all that he has. We will experience being co-glorified with him provided that we accept his sufferings as our own.

As heirs of God through Christ, we are entitled to inherit all that He has. Now we know that God is infinite in power, and everything on heaven and earth belongs to Him. It is difficult to imagine that everything good belongs to us through heirship and the sacrifice of Jesus! But this was included on the cross, and to neglect this section of scripture is to cut the power of the cross short.

All that the Father has is available to us. This includes health, wholeness, victory, peace of mind, security, faith, joy, and so much more. It also includes finances, homes, land, money to pay your bills, and so much more! This all sounds wonderful. We may think, *But how do we get in position to receive all of this,* because we may not feel like heirs of God and joint heirs with Christ. It takes faith and knowing who we are in Him. Who are we identifying as? *When we know who we are and we are confident in our position as children of God, then we will believe that we are heirs to all He has for us.* Therefore, we must find ourselves in Him as His children. We are heirs, and Jesus already died and rose again, putting into effect our status as receivers of all He has and is.

I love the Passion Translation footnote *a* on this scripture. It states, "Grace has made former rebels into princes and princesses, royal ones that share in the inheritance of Christ." If we go back to Chapter 1 where we looked at the prodigal son, we see again one son who knew what belonged to him (the one that left) and one that stayed but didn't understand his inheritance. He was faithful to his father but didn't understand that what his father owned was his, and because of this, he worked and toiled as a servant would while all along he was the owner. It all belonged to him. Let's not be like the son who threw away and took for granted his inheritance, but let's also not be like the son who lived like a servant and ignored his inheritance. Everything the Father is and has belongs to us. Let's make sure that in life, we understand that as His children, we are entitled to it. Let us not get so caught up in the "work" of being a Christian that we forget the "reward."

Knowing our heirship also enables us to use our authority. When we understand our positioning as children of God and our rights as heirs of God and joint heirs with Christ, then we will understand the authority we have in this life. Luke 10:19 states:

> Now you understand that I have imparted to you all my authority to trample over his (Satan's) kingdom. You will trample upon every demon before you and overcome every power Satan possesses. Absolutely nothing will be able to harm you as you walk in this authority.

We have been given all authority over the enemy. Just as the Father gave all authority to Jesus, Jesus gave all authority to us! Authority is the "legal right to command or to act." Jesus gave us the legal right over Satan. *Then why do I feel so defeated in life?* we may ask. Because we do not know who we are. We are self-identifying incorrectly and missing all the rights and benefits of being a child of God. But when we know in full our rights, our authority, our heirship, and who we are, then we become unstoppable. And this is detrimental to the kingdom of Satan. A church who knows who they are because of whose they are is a "church not having spot or wrinkle" (Ephesians 5:27 NKJV). Are we feeling empowered yet? I hope so. Because a Christian that identifies and knows their full rights and authority is a powerhouse believer of Christ, and nothing can stop them!

CHAPTER 7

—— ✦ ——

I cannot finish this book without speaking about the blessing. As children of God, we must understand the power of the blessing in our lives. When hearing the word *blessing*, many people think about an object or a gift. For example, one might say, "I received a gift card from my neighbor today. Oh, what a blessing!" And while that is not necessarily an incorrect usage of the word *blessing*, it does downgrade the power of what that word truly embodies.

Blessing in the Bible was not used to identify an object or thing, but it was a word of empowerment spoken over someone—a covenant. When speaking about the blessing, we must look at one of our Old Testament forefathers, Abraham. Abraham is definitely one that we associate with the blessing. In fact, many of us have heard of the Abrahamic Blessing or Covenant. In Genesis 12:3 (NKJV), God is speaking to Abram (pre-Abraham), and He says "I will bless those who bless you, and I will curse those that curse you," and here it is, "And in you all the families of the earth shall be blessed." That should get us excited! I am a part of a family in the earth, and that means I AM BLESSED. We are included in this scripture! We may not fully know what that means until we study it out, but the fact that we are blessed means that we are empowered to prosper.

In the Old Testament, when we see someone being "blessed," we do not see them just given natural possessions, but we see a word of empowerment and success spoken over them. For example, in Genesis 24:60, we read of Rebekah's mom and brother blessing her before giving her over as wife to Isaac. They didn't give her possessions, but they spoke an empowerment over her, "and they blessed

Rebekah and said to her." That is the blessing—a word spoken over someone that empowers them to prosper. Blessing requires some deep studying of the Word, which we should be encouraged to do as we are a part of this empowerment!

The blessing on Abraham made everything he did turn to good. When we watch the life of Abraham, we see the hand of God work on His behalf. This is what the blessing does for us. As children of God, co-heirs with Christ, we are also recipients of the blessing of Abraham. Therefore, everything we do should turn to good. When we know who we are in Christ and we identify as children of God, then the promises of Deuteronomy 28:1–14 become ours to claim! It is when we do not understand this covenant with Abraham and understand that we, too, are a part of this covenant, we fail to believe that we are entitled to the blessing. We are receivers of this empowerment.

Proverbs 10:22 (NKJV) declares, "The blessing of the Lord makes one rich, and He adds no sorrow with it." Rich can be defined as earthly possessions, and that is, in my opinion, accurate. But I do not believe we can limit it to that. I believe rich means content with earthly possessions but also full in our heart and soul. I knew a person who had an abundance of earthly possessions. They were rich. They owned much land and houses, and they lacked for nothing. However, these people had no peace. They were in fear of losing what they did have, they were physically constantly fighting battles in their health, and they were not content in life. I would not call that rich. Wealthy, maybe, but not rich. To be rich is to be content with an abundance in every aspect of life. It is to be full of love, peace, health, and yes, material possessions. *To be rich is to abound in life, and the blessing or empowerment spoken over us makes us abound in life.*

The blessing is passed from generation to generation. However, if we do not understand our position in this blessing, as children of God, then we won't take advantage of it in our lives. If we do not take advantage of it in our lives, then most likely, we will not pass this knowledge and understanding to our next generation. And instead of living in the fullness of God, we will just get by with what we do know of. I always say if the Bible says I can have it, then I want to know about it, and I want to implement it in my life so that I can pass it on to my children! You can't enjoy what you don't know you have. If I was an heir to a million dollars and it sat in a bank account waiting on me but I never knew I had it, then it will do me no good. It is when we know what we have that we are able to use it. When we know whose we are and WHO we are, then we will be able to go through life living in the fullness of being a child of God.

Many times in life, my husband and I have been called lucky. *Everything always seems to work out in your favor*, we have been told. We just smile and say, "It's the blessing working on our behalf." When we take our eyes off Jesus and off who He has made us to be, then we forget what has been given to us. We forget that we have been empowered to prosper. That everything we put our hand to do SHOULD work out. Then we begin to turn to God and question Him as if He has lifted His hand off of our lives. But it is in the daily business that we forget to invoke the blessing of God over everything we do and say. We should daily remind ourselves, *I am part of the spiritual lineage of Abraham and a partaker in the blessing spoken over Him.* More importantly, *I am an heir of God and a joint-heir with Christ. I am a child of God and therefore, everything He has belongs to me! I am blessed to be a blessing or empowered to empower! Everything the Bible says I can have, I have in Jesus's name!* And then, speak Deuteronomy 28:1–14 over your life! The more we say it, the more it gets into our spirit, and we believe it. The more we believe it, the more it will become evident in our lives!

CONCLUSION

I pray that this book has opened our eyes to who we truly are. We are more than mere humans just trying to get by and do good in this life. We are sons and daughters of the Most High God. We are heirs of Him and all He has and is. We have an identity, and with it comes authority and acceptance. We are free from sin and the effects of sin in our lives. We have an association with the heavenlies, and we are accepted by God! We hold ourselves to a standard of a child of God, and we will accept nothing less than His best in our lives! We are not lost, but we are found in Him. And we are confident in His love and mercy toward us. We are loved and treasured by God.

When God sees us, He sees us through Jesus. Jesus cascades over us and covers us with His love. God does not judge us based on what we do or don't do. He judges us based on what Jesus did! We are righteous because He is righteous! We are free from sickness and disease, and it has no power over us. We are called and will fulfill that calling in our lives because WE KNOW WHO WE ARE. Our identity is in HIM! Daily we must remind ourselves of this. We should look ourselves in the mirror every day and declare His Word over our lives.

The world is depending on believers who know who they are in Christ to reach them. But if we are living life defeated by guilt, shame, and death, then we will not be effective as a Christian. It is time for the church to identify as His body and know who we are. It is time to rise up in the fullness of Jesus and take this world for Him. Our neighbor needs a Christian who knows their identity. Our family needs a believer who understand their authority in Christ. This world needs a body that isn't riddled with shame or arguing over the nitty gritty of "Christian living" but a body that is strong and confident in their identity as The Body of Christ! We cannot sit by and act like the world. Rise up, children of God, and let us take our place in this world. Answer His call. Be victorious! Know who we are!

REFERENCES

All Bible texts are from The Passion Translation (Biblegateway.com), unless otherwise noted.

Chapter 1, Paragraph 2: Luke 15
Chapter 1, Paragraph 4: Luke 10:19, Psalm 24:1
Chapter 1, Paragraph 6: Exodus 16:3 NKJV
Chapter 1, Paragraph 10: Psalm 16:10
Chapter 2, Paragraph 2: John 1:46 (TPT Footnote)
Chapter 2, Paragraph: 2 Acts 2:7
Chapter 2, Paragraph 3: Matthew 13:55–57
Chapter 2, Paragraph 3: Billy Graham footnote, Winner, Lauren F. Farm Boy: How Billy Graham Became a Preacher, https://www.christianitytoday.com/ct/2018/billy-graham/billy-graham-childhood-farm-north-carolina.html
Chapter 2, Paragraph 4: Tsai, Shan P et al. "Age at retirement and long-term survival of an industrial population: prospective cohort study." BMJ (Clinical research ed.) vol. 331,7523 (2005): 995. doi:10.1136/bmj.38586.448704.E0
Chapter 3, Paragraph 1: 1 Peter 2:9
Chapter 3, Paragraph 1: www.webstersdictionary1828.com/Dictionary/chosen
Chapter 3, Paragraph 1: John 15:16
Chapter 3, Paragraph 2: 2 Corinthians 1:21a
Chapter 3, Paragraph 3: 2 Corinthians 5:21
Chapter 3, Paragraph 4: www.webstersdisctionary1828.com/Dictionary/communion

Chapter 3, Paragraph 4: Isaiah 43:1 NKJV

Chapter 4, Paragraph 1: www.webstersdictionary1828.com/dictionary/redemption

Chapter 4, Paragraph 1: 1 Corinthians 15:55–56

Chapter 4, Paragraph 2: Matthew 8:24

Chapter 4, Paragraph 4: Isaiah 53:5 TPT & NKJV

Chapter 4, Paragraph 4: 2 Corinthians 5:17 & Footnote (a)

Chapter 4, Paragraph 4: Ephesians 1:7

Chapter 5, Paragraph 1: www.webstersdictionary1828/dictionary/grace

Chapter 5, Paragraph 1: 2 Corinthians 5:21

Chapter 5, Paragraph 1: 2 Corinthians 12:9

Chapter 5, Paragraph 2: Ephesians 1:5–6 (TPT), and Verse 6 NKJV

Chapter 5, Paragraph 3: 2 Peter 1:3

Chapter 5, Paragraph 4: Hebrews 13:5

Chapter 6, Paragraph 1: Romans 3:24–26

Chapter 6, Paragraph 1: www.webstersdictionary1828.com/dictionary/acquittal

Chapter 6, Paragraph 3: Psalm 37:4

Chapter 6, Paragraph 3: Philippians 4: 19

Chapter 6, Paragraph 4: www.webstersdictionary1828/dictionary/heir

Chapter 6, Paragraph 4: Romans 8:17 and TPT Footnote (a)

Chapter 6, Paragraph 5: Luke 10:19

Chapter 6, Paragraph 5: www.webstersdictionary1828.com/dictionary/authority

Chapter 6, Paragraph 5: Eph. 5:27 NKJV

Chapter 7, Paragraph 1: Genesis 12:3 NKJV

Chapter 7, Paragraph 1: Gen 24:60 NKJV

Chapter 7, Paragraph 3: Proverbs 10:22 NKJV